Help!
I Married a Quilter

Mark Hyland

Help!
I Married a Quilter

Mark Hyland

Quilters Touch, LLC

Cottonwood Heights, Utah

Helpful suggestions and edits were done by my wife, The Quilter. How else could I answer other than "Yes Dear" when asked, "Would you like some suggestions and helpful hints?"

A portion of the proceeds from the sale of this book will be donated to charities associated with quilts or quilting.

ISBN 978-0-9790075-1-4

First Printing 2006

Printed in the United States of America

TABLE OF CONTENTS

OH, I FORGOT TO TELL YOU SOMETHING ABOUT MYSELF

PREFACE

THE REALIZATION

*I*n 1989 my wife and I were married after a short courtship and engagement. I was in love! Everything was wonderful and grand. Not a care in the world. It was exciting and new.

Immediately after our wedding ceremony, as we were exiting the building, my new father-in-law asked if he could speak to me briefly prior to some family photos.

Inside I am thinking, *"What can Dad possibly want to speak to me about right now?"* Well, I soon found out.

First you need to understand something about my father-in-law. He is a great man (*and I am not just saying that to gain some inheritance*), quiet-spoken, wise, and dedicated to his family. He had already spoken to my wife and I during our engagement. He promised that he would never give us advice or interfere unless we asked.

As Dad pulled me aside, he began, "I want to give you some advice …."

I am thinking, *"NOW? Right after the ceremony? People are waiting on us for pictures... Hey, wait a minute... I don't remember **asking** for this advice."*

However, all I could do was gulp a faint smile and listen. Dad looked me right in the eye and with a very solemn, fatherly look on his face continued, "Son, there are two words that will make your life much more enjoyable now that you are married. They are YES DEAR." And with that all important wisdom, delivered with a blow, he smiled, turned, and walked away, leaving me, the newly wed, completely caught off guard and not sure what to think.

I walked with a little less confidence than before over to

the waiting picture parade. My wife asked me a question that I can't remember but I remember my answer... *"YES DEAR."*

What I didn't understand at that moment, was that with those two little words, I no longer had control of my life. My wife did.

After I realized that my wife had complete control, I started to notice that my life was heading in a direction that I had not planned or even dared imagine. You see, I soon found out that my wife liked to quilt. A harmless little hobby I thought. Stitching pretty little blankets. How nice. I soon realized, however, that she liked to quilt so much that it became part of her identity, albeit an identity I wasn't fully aware of before marriage. I soon started to refer to her affectionately as "The Quilter." And every so often, OK, I mean every other day, she would need to buy some supplies for a new project and of course I would say, "Yes Dear."

My father-in-law's advice was making for a very happy marriage. But I had a few more lessons to learn. I think, possibly, that saying *Yes Dear* to an ordinary woman may not be that catastrophic. It probably really works great. But when you say *Yes Dear* too many times to a woman who loves to quilt, you have headed down a path from which there is no return.

It all became crystal clear one day when The Quilter said, "Honey, on Tuesday night some of the quilt group is coming over to put some quilts together for Project Linus."

Of course my trained unsarcastic response was, *"Yes Dear."* (See Dad! I learned my lesson well.)

It wasn't until Tuesday evening when I saw that my home was being turned into a light manufacturing facility that I REALIZED that I had really and truly been overtaken by quilts, quilters, and quilting.

There was no control left to be had. It had long since vanished. There was no possibility of gaining any control back. Every bit of ground that I had lost to quilting was gone forever. I seriously, at one point, thought of staging a coup. But I knew that would never work because I was hopelessly in love with the enemy.

No. Quilting was here to stay. It had become a life-force pulsating through the Quilter that would never die. It also grows, multiplies, and then spreads like a virus to every person the Quilter knows. And soon the Quilter's friends swarm into your home to create a hive of quilting madness.

On this particular evening, my home, my castle, my haven, had morphed into a quilt factory. I was soon sucked into the vortex of activity, moving furniture to accommodate more arrivals. It was just as I imagined a sweatshop to be.

The kitchen had been transformed into a large staging room with cutting mats strewn across the kitchen table. All types and brands of sewing machines were set up makeshift-like on extra banquet tables in the living room and family room. Sergers were screaming along as the chatting quilters pushed continuous yardage of fabric through their machines. Batting, scraps of fabric, and varieties of thread were everywhere. And just when I thought that the controlled chaos was at its peak, the chime of the door bell would echo in the distance and another quilter would arrive. More room was made . . .

Now those of you that have experienced this in your own home will know that quilters don't just bring the bare essentials, they bring everything that they remotely, possibly, could use. Plus, they absolutely need to bring their latest project to share!

I am not sure, how many machines we carried in that night or how many of "the group" showed up. But as I watched each person leave and promise to get together and do this again *"real soon"* my future flashed before my eyes and I knew that I was into this for keeps. I was truly past the point of **NO RETURN.**

Several months later while walking around a quilting show in Duluth, Minnesota I was hit with this thought: "I am 800 miles

away from home, walking a quilting show on the weekend
when I could be doing a 100 different (dare I say more manly?)
things".

What had happened? It was The Quilter and I was completely
under her spell. At that precise moment I knew what I had to
do. I needed to capture these quilting experiences and share
them. Not for me, but for others who may still have a chance to
survive.

The title of this book suddenly came to me as I watched
all the quilters in their excited and frenzied state patrol the
show floor . . . I dared not say the words out loud because I
was afraid I would shout at the top of my lungs right then and
there....

HELP! I Married a Quilter.

The following pages contain a glance into the life of quilting,
or should I say being married to a quilter. This is a comedic,
yet surprisingly realistic look at the quirks and idiosyncrasies
of quilters in general. After all, truth can be stranger and even
funnier than fiction. These are my observations over several
years of marriage to The Quilter. My wonderful wife, The Quilter, comes from a long line of quilters. Five generations in fact!
(Do you think I even stood a chance?)

I am not completely alone, fortunately. Most of the experiences offered here are mine, but I also offer similar tales of woe,
gathered from many others who have that same terrified look in
their eye that cries *"HELP!"*

If you are married to a quilter, these observations, situations,
and stories will affirm many of the realities and challenges you
face. If *you* are a quilter, then maybe these pages will give you
another perspective on how your chosen lifestyle affects those
around you. People you love, like your husband, are willing to

sacrifice a lot, including a fair amount of their common sense and sanity to help you maintain this little habit of yours.

I have often thought of forming a therapeutic guild or society for us spouses of quilters. Then the thought quickly fades as I wonder when I would have the time with all the quilting nights, shows, and meetings or just helping with the next project. The familiar and humorous anecdotes found in these pages may be the only therapy I can offer you.

For those of you who are new to this wacky world of quilting, with its secret language, guild meetings, shop hops, forums, new gadgets, and special sales, this is meant as a wake up call to make sure you have a clearer understanding of the inner-most workings of the quilter, before it becomes too late.

You see, the quilter in your life is *going* to win. Yes. She really does love you, but quilting is something she just has to do. Ask-ing her to cut back or quit is like asking her to stop breathing... or shopping. Don't fight it, just learn and adjust.

On a serious note, I am often kidded by my colleagues and friends that I really know too much about quilting, which is probably true, compared to the layperson. However, through the years, I have come to respect, admire, and stand in awe at the talent and dedication of a quilter. To The Quilter, it is an expression of love and warmth passed down from generation to generation. A quilt communicates this affection in ways that a mere blanket just won't.

If you have not been to a quilt show, it may be worth your time to attend, even if its just for the brownie points – I know I always need some. There are truly some amazing and gifted art-ists in the world of quilting. And the love and camaraderie they feel for each other and the genuine interest they show in each other's projects is quite inspiring.

OK! Enough of this adoration and on to the real reason for this book!

I have to admit, I have never attempted to quilt and probably never will. It could be that I do not have the patience for it or it could be that I know that I do not possess the talent. Never-the-less, quilters are a breed unto themselves. It is difficult to pick them out of a crowd and you are often surprised that they are quilters when you do find out. You will never look at them in the same light again, trust me.

I must also mention, however, that you can easily pick out the spouse of a quilter. It's someone like me, trying to be supportive, standing in a corner of the fabric or quilt shop with a dumbfounded glazed look on his face saying, "Not another project!" When I see them, we may exchange a quick nod of understanding as if to say, "I completely understand what you are going through. Hang in there brother." Every now and then I will also see a new face of someone being dragged to their first quilt shop. All I can do is shake my head and walk on by. He will learn soon enough.

HI, I'M MARK AND I'M MARRIED TO A QUILTER

ARE YOU MARRIED TO A QUILTER?

You ask, "Who is a quilter"?

The answer may not be as easy as you may think. The simple concept or definition is: One who makes quilts. This conjures up thoughts of Great Grandma slowly rocking back in forth in her well-worn turn-of-the-century rocking chair with thimble and thread in hand, carefully and tenderly stitching the delicate fabric draped across her lap. Or it may be thoughts of Mom putting the quilting racks up in the basement in preparation for her newest project. Maybe your spouse puts quilting frames up in your living room for days at a time.

So when does someone who quilts every now and again become a *QUILTER?* How will you know when she has crossed over and changed her identity from "I like to quilt sometimes," to "I'M A QUILTER!" This in reality, as it turns out, is not as simple as you think. Yes, quilters are your friends and neighbors, those you work with, or the check-out clerk at your favorite grocery store, or even an acquaintance at your civic group. In regular circles they appear so...normal. The reality is this: A quilter is a very complex multi-faceted individual with many qualities and attributes. So let's start at the very beginning, as it is very a good place to start.

Each of us who has attempted to understand the wild world of quilting is continually mystified by the complexity of what we thought was a simple thing. I remember my grandmother putting together quilts while I was growing up. Grandma Rose would set up a quilt frame, have a few friends over, and tie a quilt in one afternoon. Piece of cake right? Wrong. A quilter's world is as simple or as complex as each individual quilter desires to make it. And just when you think you have it figured out, whammy, it changes.

It usually starts with a change in purchasing habits. You will find that your sensible partner has started buying fabric that she is going to use "someday." Then she starts buying needed equipment, frames, newfangled sewing machines, etc. etc. Then her schedule changes. She starts attending regular quilting bees, shows, and meetings. And it goes on and on.

I myself have to admit that I know way too much about the whole process and what a quilter does and thinks. That in and of itself is a pretty scary notion. For those of you who may not have as much experience or interaction with a quilter, the following questionnaire is to help you assess the damage or hope that may currently exist for you. For those of you who are currently living with a quilter but are acting like an ostrich (burying your head in the sand so you can pretend it does not exist), these questions will help you accurately determine where you are in the quilting cycle and what, if anything, you can do about it.

The follow questions have been prepared in a simple yes or no questionnaire format. They are not given to frighten you. They are here to help you, so you can adjust to your new life. However, there are some ground rules to help you best assess your own dilemma or condition.

1 – DO NOT in any circumstances allow your quilter to influence your choices. This questionnaire is best taken when she is away at a quilting function.

2 – Answer the questions honesty and openly. If you don't know the correct answer, it is probably to your benefit.

3 – Do NOT over-think the question. They really are *SEW* simple. . .

4 – NEVER show the results to your quilter. This could be very detrimental to your cause, unless there is absolutely no hope for you, and then you might get some sympathy.

5 – Keep score! "Yes" equals the number of points shown on the question. "No" equals zero points for that question.

Good LUCK, I hope this turns out better for you than it did for me.

Are YOU Married to a Quilter?

Part One – Spending Habits and Asset Inventory

a. Has your spouse shopped at more than three different quilt shops in the last six weeks?
   One point.

b. Has your spouse ever called you from a quilt store to ask how much money is available in checking and savings?
   One point.

c. Does your spouse have special times that she must go to the fabric store to get their special monthly sale? One point.

d. Do the local quilt shops send your wife Christmas cards? Birthday cards? One point each.

e. Do you consistently ask yourself *"what now"* when she comes home from the fabric store? One point.

f. Has your spouse ever purchased fabric on a vacation? One point.

g. Have you ever had to buy an extra bag on vacation to bring home the fabric she bought? Two points.

h. Does you wife have a sewing machine? Two? Three? One point for each machine.

i. Does your spouse own a serger? One point.

j. Does your spouse have a cutting table? One point.

k. Does your spouse own a long-arm quilting machine? Two points.

l. Is your wife willing to drive the old *Buick* for five more years so she can buy another quilting or sewing machine? Two points.

m. Do you have more that three yards of fabric in your home? One point.

n. Does your spouse have enough fabric in her stash to open her own store? Two points

Part Two – Personal Schedule and Memberships

a. Does your spouse belong to a quilt guild, society, or group? One point.

b. Is your spouse an officer in any of these groups? Two points.

c. Does she attend a regularly scheduled quilting function every month? One point for each meeting.

d. Has your spouse ever been to a Quilt Show? One point.

e. Has your spouse ever displayed a quilt at a quilt show or exhibit? One point for each quilt.

f. Has she been to the quilting venues in Paducah, Kentucky or Houston, Texas? Two points.

Part Three – Daily Life and Relationships

a. Does your spouse currently have more that three quilt projects going? One point for each project over three.

b. Does she quilt in the car, in waiting rooms, while watching TV, or while visiting friends on a portable quilting hoop? One point.

c. Does your wife's quilting affect the quality of the family meals? One point. (If your answer is yes, NEVER tell your spouse.)

d. Does she have a separate sewing room or studio? One point for a room, two points for a studio.

e. Does your quilter always have threads hanging off her clothing? One point

f. Have you ever been awoken in the morning to a quilting
   show on TV? One point.

g. Do you check your schedule around your wife's quilting
   schedule? One point.

Just one more part to the survey, and it may be the most important
part. The degree which your spouse has involved you in this whole
quilting addiction will tell you really how far gone you are.

Part Four – How Much are You Involved?

a. Have you been to a quilt store with your spouse? One point.

b. Have you ever helped with the purchase? (Carrying fabric
   to the cutting table counts.) Two points.

c. Is there a category for quilting supplies in the family budget? Two points.

d. Have *YOU* been to a quilt show? Two points.

e. Have *YOU* been to Paducah, Kentucky or Houston, Texas
   with your quilter? Three points.

f. Have *YOU* watched a quilting TV program with your
   spouse? One point. By yourself? Two points.

g. Do you know what a "fat quarter" is? One point.

h. Have you ever cut a fat quarter? Two points.

i. Have *YOU* ever quilted? Three points.

Finished? Good. Whatever you do, don't go back and re-read your responses, it may only make you depressed. Now, if you have completed all of the questions, add up your points and write the number down.

You may have noticed that some questions are worth more than others. Well, that goes without saying, some items are just more telling than others. As in the title of this chapter, your point value will tell you if you are married to a *QUILTER* or just to someone who likes to quilt every now and then. (For now.)

Less than 10 points – You are a Lucky Man.

Your spouse may just like to quilt every now and again, maybe just to be social with her quilting friends. You are the envy of all of us quilting spouses. Just remember we all started where you are now at one time. Be watchful for signs – never underestimate the ability of her friends to infect her with the quilting virus. The transformation from **You're a Lucky Man status to *Goner*** can be as quick as stitch'n in the ditch.

11 to 20 points – Be on Guard.

Your spouse has definitely been bitten. The disease may still be in the incubation period, so she still may recover and come to her senses. It really depends a lot on you. If you are super supportive *(Yes Dear)* and let her hang out with quilters and shop at any quilt shop that pops up, then the sickness may really set in. Be watchful of fabric sales… they'll put you into the next category as fast as a Pfaff "switches stitches". (Say that 10 time fast, if you can–you're already in the next category). But if you exercise some tough love and restrict her spending and quilting activities she might recover and be happy stitching only now and again as in the Lucky Man category above. Good luck trying to restrict her spending–it will probably never happen.

21 to 30 points – Hunker Down

You're delusional if you think that this will pass as a fad. It's now in her blood! Maybe a transfusion would work. Just make sure it's not from another quilter. I will be honest. I have never seen the quilting bug go into remission at this stage. If you are fortunate you may be able to keep her at this stage by giving her a Nordstrom credit card with no spending limit. This may divert her attention for long enough periods of time to keep her from advancing to the next level. Of course my wife claims that quilting is cheaper than therapy, and it may be cheaper than unlimited spending at Nordstrom.

31 to 40 points – Not much HOPE

Once you are at this level and beyond there is really no going back. All you can do is try to hold your own and try to keep the illness in quarantine. Keep as many of your old traditions as possible. Encourage your quilter to quilt while you fish or watch a football game. She isn't going to watch the game with you but you will at least be in the same room. You must, at this point, emotionally adjust to the fact that the last thing your spouse will do in this life is make one last stitch in her latest project.

41 to 50 – Join In (or at least pretend too)

The realization hits... nothing will stop the quilt projects from adding up...12, 13, 14, and that is just the number in production. At this stage it doesn't even have to be on sale. Any passing want becomes a deep-seeded NEED. It is now time to pick only one part of your life that you want to hold onto. The rest will have to go. You have become the quilter's assistant, chauffeur, and business manager. Yes, your quilter by this time has started thinking that going into business will help pay the bills.

50 plus points – GONER

If you are in this category, then you already know it. You lead a double life. You don't let anyone at the office know about the condition of things at home. You check the internet for sport scores and then pretend you saw the game if someone asks. You went shopping at Cabela's or Best Buy; not a Quilt shop. C'mon! Also, your wife can't come to the party on Friday because.... she broke her leg! You never admit that she can't come to the annual company party because someone foolishly planned it on her quilt night. You have my deepest sympathy. But also know that you are not alone.

ENOUGH IS ENOUGH...
IS NEVER REALLY ENOUGH

During our courtship, many years ago, I remember my wife discussing with her mother that she was a fifth generation quilter. I thought, "Wow! That is kinda cool." Little did I know at the time what that really meant. Because my future wife was a quilter by heredity there was so much of the genetic characteristics built up from the previous generations that I stood no chance of having a non-quilting wife. But hey, I was a glassy-eyed young man that was clueless to what being married to a quilter would really be like.

It may be a good idea to look into the past generations to determine if you are fighting against heredity. Although the awakening within may lie dormant for many years, let me assure you when the urge occurs, the urgency increases, and the quilter is off and moving full-steam ahead.

And when your wife has made the plunge and started quilting there is another event that occurs which should scare anyone who is trying to maintain fiscal sanity. It is the need for all quilters to acquire supplies. Now, if you have been thinking that quilting consists of a simple needle and thread and some scraps of fabric you are sadly mistaken. They have not yet begun to invent all of the gadgets that your quilter cannot live without.

I am sure many of you have been watching TV when one of those infomercials or TV brand commercials appear. It is always some new and exciting product that the world can not do without, especially you the consumer. (Or so they make you think.) You know the ones I am referring too:

> *"Ever wonder how to get that stain out of your carpet, dress, kitchen counter, dog, golf bag.... Well now there is a way. The amazing Stain Depleter System does it for you. For only $19.95 you will never have*

a stain again! You can not get rid of ....yadda yadda yadda."

Just as you are ready to zap to the next channel, the hook line resonates through your brain as a command:

"But WAIT THERE'S MORE . . . For the next 100 callers who order the New Amazing Handy Dandy Stain Depleter they will get ABSOLUTELY FREE, one years' worth of Amazing Handy Dandy Stain Depleter personal sticks, a $49.95 Value... But Wait, there's more: for the first 10 callers who act right now and order, will also receive absolutely free (pause, big pause) a 100 piece set of steak knives. . .just in case you invite 100 friends over for steak. Call now, do not delay" (or in other words get this before your friend does).

Well this informercial is not too far off explaining the transformation that somehow occurs in the quilting mind when it realizes that there is something new out there that the quilter must have. The only difference is that the "Wait! There's more," is *never* free.

You can prepare for the inevitable depletion of funds if you can recognize the different stages that your quilter will go through before having to make a purchase. It won't stop the purchase, it will only delay it for a while until you can mortgage something.

The first stage is "The Gaze": It's that look. You know the one, just like the anticipation on children's faces at a toy or candy store when they suddenly realize that they might be able to purchase their favorite toy or candy. There is no way to completely explain it, but I guarantee that you will experience it. When you do, you'll recognize "the gaze" just as you recognize "the look" you get from your spouse or significant other when you have crossed the line.

The Gaze is very real and very noticeable. If you catch it quickly, you may have the ability to prevent it (for a time) from going on to the next stage.

The second stage consists of Facial Smirks of Expressions: Although not as obvious as The Gaze, Facial Smirks usually occur several moments after the gaze has concluded. If you are very observant you will see the slightest up-turn at the corner of the mouth, the eyes twinkle and become enlarged with almost a frantic look of resolution.

What has just occurred is a very realistic fantasy that the quilter has just purchased the sought after item and it is in their possession *right now.* They will hold this expression for quite a while before the smile fades as they begin to realize that they *do not* have this much needed quilting item...*yet.*

The next stage is what I call "Twitchynessless." Only the trained eye will catch this significant event. Watch carefully as this event takes a while to set in. Twitchynessless is my word. It is the cross between fidgety, anxiousness, and being restless. Let me explain. When a quilter has mentally already purchased an item, (see the second stage), then not having the item becomes a very difficult matter. Everywhere the quilter looks, that item is missing. It should be there, after all, the quilter has seen it in the reality of her own fantasy. This magically transforms this *quilting want* into a *genuine need*... like air. Doing without the item creates twitchynessless. It will not stop. It will only get worse. If for some absolutely normal reason it happens to turn out to be an expensive item, then you really should hurry and arrange your finances accordingly.

The last stage of acquisition is what I call Happy Hands. It is the culmination of the other three steps. The purchase has been made and the quilter's hands busily dig into making use of this new item. You feel relieved, your quilter is happy and satisfied, caught up in her quilting project. Life is good and there is joy with your quilter once more. You settle back to enjoy this moment looking over at your quilter as "The Gaze" reappears.

The cycle will repeat over and over because there will never be enough of anything for a quilter. In future chapters we will discuss the fabric "stash" that each quilter will spend a lifetime acquiring. My wife has enough fabric to last through generations six and seven *and* part of generation eight. Also, why must they always be buying the latest gadget and machine? There is an answer to that question, I am told. I am just not sure I believe it.

Enough is enough is never enough doesn't even say it quite well enough. A true quilter does not have the word *ENOUGH* in her vocabulary.

SURE WE CAN AFFORD IT, HONEY. I JUST SOLD
YOUR GOLF CLUBS AND THE LAWN MOWER ON ebay.

QUILTERS ARE LIKE GOLFERS
(THEY JUST DON'T KNOW IT)

I am going to make an assumption, and I try not to make assumptions as it usually gets me in trouble. However in this case I assume that at least some of you are golfers or at least have golfed or have been into a golf shop. Some of you may be serious weekend golfers, others are probably good hackers like me, and maybe some of you are very good golfers as well. However, I am sure that we all know someone who is a serious golfer or who is seriously into golf.

I learned some time ago from the CEO of a major golf manufacturer that golfers are the easiest individuals to market to for one simple fact. They are always looking for a quick or easy fix to improve their game. Sound familiar?

If you improve any part of their game – correcting a slice, driving the ball longer, getting out of the sand, faster head speed, better trajectory – you can sell it. According to this executive it was simple. Continue to come up with new products or improvements to existing products that will help golfers meet there continually changing *needs* and you will always be successful.

If the person you are thinking of is anything like the golfer I know, he always has a new club, a different type of ball, a new something-or-other to improve his game. Does it work? Sometimes, or a least he thinks it does.

The golfing industry perpetuates this need for additional items that the average golfer can't do without through many specific magazines. There's *Golfer, Senior Golf, Golf Inc, Golfers World, Golfer's Workshop, Golfer Weekly, Junior Golfer, The PGA,* etc. These magazines promote golf accessories like old-time peddlers selling elixir from the back of a wagon. And intelligent people line up and buy it.

The worst thing of all is meeting with a golfer at the pro shop prior to a round of golf. I know, I have done it. Whatever the latest challenge was with this guy's game, we had to find some help. If it was putting, it was probably the putter. I think he tried every putter in the place and even took one out as a demo. Did he putt better that day? It really didn't matter, if the putter felt better and the golfer thought it improved his putting ability, it was worth the purchase. Most of the time it didn't matter what the price tag was.

New golf balls that provided 20 extra yards with better control, $38 per dozen, no problem. A $32.50 golf glove for better grip, the $140 sand wedge guaranteed to get you out of the toughest trap, or the $29 golf visor were all considered wise investments in this all important game. There are never ending possibilities of what can be marketed to golfers who are seriously into golf.

Well, quilters are a lot like Golfers, only worse. I don't know why they are worse, it just feels that way. They are really quite similar.

In golf you will hopefully improve your game through tons of practice and repetitive action. A decent set of clubs and a lot of practice should do the trick. Right? After all, that's all Tiger Woods had.

In quilting you improve over time with a little practice and coaching. A good needle and thread and some decent fabric is all you need. After all, that's all Grandma had. Right?

Oh, no! Just like golf, quilting has entered the 21st Century with a vengeance. And it doesn't matter if your spouse is a hand quilter or a machine quilter, there are new and improved items to be found at the quilter's *Pro Shop*. OK, now I remember why quilters are worse than golfers. A good golf shop will carry almost every new thing for the golfer. A quilter on the other hand has to go to three or twelve different shops to find all of the latest stuff.

To me, hand quilters are the most difficult of all quilters to understand. Here is why. They will still spend a fortune on all of the latest needles, threads, scissors, thimbles, finger-cots, gloves, cutting tools, patterns, etc. etc. etc. just to do things as *slowly* as grandma did. They just do it with a lot more style. They are the purists. Oh yeah, purists with laser sharpened platinum needles, razor-sharp rotary cutting blades, computerized cutting boards, specially made Civil War era style fabric and thread, and book after magazine after book showing you how to make quilts the old-fashioned way. Grandma would not be able to keep up.

Then there are the machine quilters. Golfers, kneel and pay homage. You can't compete with this group. What would take Grandma six months can now be done in an afternoon. Grandma practiced and practiced to get 14 stitches per inch, but heck plug in your new mid-arm quilting machine with a computerized stitch regulator and you can have Grandma beat on your first try.

Even your grandma had a sewing machine. But hers was nothing like the computerized mini-factories that sewing machines are today. Every stitch known to man is available at the touch of a button. And if you need a special stitch just upload it onto your programmable system. I could be exaggerating but I swear that I have seen a sewing machine that can make a tuxedo after pushing just one button.

Machine-quilters want/NEED every new sewing gadget there is. Hence, some quilters will own three to four to six different specialty sewing machines. There are electronic bobbin winders, gadget upon gadget, and of course book after magazine after book to show you how to make a complete quilt before your husband can finish the back nine.

And as cool as each of these machines are, they get better every year. You have to buy the upgrades, get all of the improvements, just so that you can make a quilt that is as nice as Grandma's.

I guess a really good comparison of hand-quilters versus machine quilters would be this. A trip from New York to London; the hand quilter would take the Queen Elizabeth II and the machine quilter would take the Concorde. In the end, they would both end up in London. Of course the machine quilter had time to see all the sites and have tea with the Queen by the time the hand quilter arrived.

In deference to the quilters referred to in this book I am going to point out where quilters *are* superior to golfers. When golfers finish a round all they have is a score to either brag or complain about. Quilters who finish a project have a work of art that can be shared and admired for generations.

Quilting Notes

A Quilting Community

Gee's Bend, Alabama is a rural area located in a bend in the Mississippi River that makes it a very difficult community to visit unless you are a quilter, then it is a pilgrimage. It was originally owned by a man named Joseph Gee and his family. He moved into the area with his family and over 100 slaves. The ownership of the land changed hands several times over the years but the slaves and their descendants stayed with the land. After the Civil War they became tenant farmers for the then current land owner by the name of Pettway, a name adopted by many of the former slaves.

The women of Gee's Bend have been quilting throughout the entire 20th century and are still renowned for maintaining this community heritage to this day. They have had numerous quilt shows and at least two very popular books printed highlighting their unique quilts and the quilting women of Gee's Bend.

Nearly every man in this community is married to a quilter. That is an amazing accomplishment in and of itself.

SOME OF THE GIRLS ARE COMING OVER TO MAKE QUILTS FOR
A FEW DAYS. CAN YOU AND THE KIDS MOVE OUT UNTIL WE'RE DONE?

THE SECRET SOCIETY OF QUILTERS

I don't know about your home, but in ours we receive an incredible amount of junk mail; credit card applications with low interest rates, realtors introducing themselves hoping for our business, grocery store ads, and the always important "to the current residents." Stuff we can't do without, right? Along with the junk mail are the bills, notices, and letters. Through the daily ritual of sorting you make sure the good mail is filed properly and the junk mail is also filed, right to the garbage.

Never make the mistake of placing the monthly announcements from the various quilting newsletters, quilting coupons, fabric shop mailings, or the *guild* flyer in that junk mail file. I tried this, once. Quilting flyers, postcards, ads, and even letters from quilting stores addressed to *occupant* are *not* junk mail! I know that now. I received a quick tutorial that day on how to sort mail, especially mail from quilt stores.

It was during one of the daily mail sorts after that incident that I noticed a friendly reminder note from one of many local quilt shops:

Don't Forget – Friday Night!
Last Friday Sampler.
Come, bring a friend!
Food, Fun, Prizes.
Door opens 8 pm.

A thought occurred. After some very quick but serious contemplation, I surprised The Quilter by saying, "Hey, why don't you take me on Friday night?"

I thought it can't be all that bad. It's late at night, can't take too long, there is food, and I can score some serious brownie points for suggesting it. Plus I am sure she will say, "That's okay honey, I'm sure you'll be bored."

This was my way out while still being supportive. Surprisingly The Quilter accepted my suggestion to go with her. Quickly my mind went into defense mode. Fake sickness! Go out of town suddenly. Break an arm. Without coming up with an excuse that would work, I was stuck.

Friday came more quickly than normal and we were off. What I now understand is that the *"Last Friday Sampler"* is better known as the *Friday Meeting of The Secret Society of Quilters.* The *Last Friday Sampler* is just a coded message from this secret society which means; we're meeting, be here, you need to see all the new stuff and new projects. It just sounds much better and doesn't clue us non-quilting spouses into the fact that quilting stuff is happening, again.

If you have never attended a *Last Friday Sampler* (the name doesn't matter. There is some sort of gathering of the *Secret Society of Quilters* everywhere. They just use different names to keep us off balance.) Let me share with you the inner working of this secret society because I was there, experienced it, and survived.

I quickly learned as we arrived that it is a requirement to bring with you "the block of the month." If not, it is difficult to gain admittance. Or "sew" it "seamed." (My wife is messing up my spelling).

I thought, "Great. No problem. Any old block will do…"

Wrong. Chalk it up to inexperience. It is a specific quilt block for that month and must be shown to gain entrance. It's really their secret password. You also need to know how to get it every month. To me it was just like the secret password I had as a kid in our neighborhood *No Girls Club* growing up. This was a sudden realization for me.

This block thing finally explained the frantic late night sounds coming from the sewing room, sorry, quilting studio, the Thursday night prior to the *Friday Night Secret Society Sampler Meeting*. This is the reason there is always a tired but satisfied look on The Quilter's face the next morning. She had the password ready.

Lucky for us on this occasion The Quilter had completed the correct block and we were admitted with no incident. I was surprised at the number of quilters that were there. There was a quiet electricity building throughout the group.

Without knowing all the correct protocol, I tried to ask how you know what block you are supposed to bring to what meeting. We were quickly asked to move to the center of the shop by one of the leaders (the shop owner). As we walked elbow to elbow with the quilters, I thought I was about to get an answer to my simple question.

Unfortunately the question was never answered because the Master of Ceremonies jumped up on the cutting table and called the meeting to attention. Deadly silence. You could hear a needle drop and there were plenty of needles in the place. The anticipation mounted, just like a large thundercloud moving over a city on a warm summer's evening.

Then without warning, it started. New quilting stuff was pulled out. Ooooos and Awwwesssss spread contagiously as items were passed around the room. Questions were asked from every corner in a coded quilter's language I did not completely understand. I held my ground and thought of a better place. Tools in my garage, Saturday afternoon football, food . . .

Sometime later, I don't know how much later, we were moving through the maze of fabric bolts going deeper and deeper into the shop.

"Wait here," I was instructed. "I need to get a look at next month's block. You know this is only a $5.00 quilt when I finish."

It must have been that blank stare on my face that signaled The Quilter that I needed further explanation.

"I paid $5.00 seven months ago for my first block. Each month when I complete my block they provide me with a kit for a new block, free. I only need 5 more blocks to finish."

There it was, the illusion of a $5.00 quilt. Because when we turned around and had to walk through all the stuff, 50 BUCKS of other stuff came home with me for the $5.00 quilt. The way I figure it, the $5.00 quilt turns into a much more expensive venture. But hey what do I know, I just try to follow directions.

I should have recognized the signs in our early years of marriage and maybe I could have stopped the fanatical quilter's itch from spreading. I doubt it, but I still can fantasize.

I now knew that my wife belonged to secret society. I was allowed to watch but I was certainly not given enough information to blow the cover off this organization. I am giving you all I know here.

The *Secret Society of Quilters* has some very significant historical background that supersedes the innocuous society of today. Prior to and during the Civil War, *The Underground Railroad* used quilts as a very secret code. Quilts were used by slaves as a message board to give instructions to each other without raising any suspicion.

This code has been preserved over time by people like Ozella Williams, an African-American woman who lives in South Carolina. She makes and sells quilts. She was told the story of the *Underground Railroad Quilt Code* by her mother and continues to tell the story to others.

The Underground Railroad Quilt Code Patterns

Monkey Wrench – *Prepare the tools you'll need for the long journey, including the mental and spiritual tools. Or (as a Ship's*

Wheel), the pilot is prepared to begin the transport.

Wagon Wheel – *Load the wagon or prepare to board the wagon to begin the escape.*

Bear's Paw – *Take a mountain trail, out of view. Follow the path made by bear tracks; they can lead you to water and food.*

Crossroads – *Refers to Cleveland, Ohio, a destination offering several routes to freedom. It also signifies reaching a point where a person's life will change, so one must be willing to go on.*

Log Cabin – *A secret symbol that could be drawn on the ground indicating that a person is safe to talk to. It also advises seeking shelter.*

Shoofly – *Possibly identifies a friendly guide who is nearby and can help.*

Bowtie – *Dress in a disguise, or put on a change of clothes.*

Flying Geese – *Points to a direction to follow, such as where geese would fly during spring migration.*

Drunkard's Path – *Create a zig-zag path, do not walk in a straight line, to avoid pursuers in this area.*

Star – *Follow the North Star. Worked in conjunction with the popular song, "Follow the Drinking Gourd," a reference to the Big Dipper constellation.*

At the time, this secret quilt code was dead serious and held the keys to liberty and life. I believe that these codes have evolved over time within the *Secret Society of Quilters.* I am not saying that I *really* know the new code, but I believe that it may go something like this.

Monkey Wrench – *Prepare the tools you'll need for your next project, including fabric and all necessary gadgets.*

Wagon Wheel – *Bring the biggest vehicle you own to this sale, preferably a large SUV or truck.*

Bear's Paw – *My husband is on to me. I will divert his attention with his favorite meal and turn on the game.*

Crossroads – *Signifies reaching a point where a quilter's life will change, making even more time available for quilting.*

Log Cabin – *A secret symbol indicating that a person is safe to talk to. This person will keep all of your quilting secrets from your husband.*

Shoofly – *Possibly identifies a friendly guide who will teach you all of the tricks and secrets of quilting.*

Bowtie – *Dress up in your best clothes so your husband will think you are going somewhere other than a quilt meeting.*

Flying Geese – *Points to a direction to follow to the nearest clearance sale. Also suggest that the early bird will be richly rewarded.*

Drunkard's Path – *Suggests that your spouse is reaching the breaking point. Create as many diversions as possible.*

Star – *Follow me to my quilt guild meeting. I will show you your new life.*

As with any secret society, most goings on are very secret, so you many not even know that your wife belongs to the *Secret Society of Quilters.* Fortunately for you I have assembled a short list of clues you can watch for. If she has indeed crossed over into that clandestine cadre of friends who will lead her down the path to Quilting Nirvana, you will know it.

Signs that you have a quilter who belongs to the *Secret Society of Quilters.*

• Although your spouse is usually directionally challenged, she can find a fabric store without ever looking up the address.

• Employees of the Quilt/Fabric Store greet your spouse by her first name in unison as she enters their store.

• Your spouse starts using new and unfamiliar words like, fat-quarter, stitch-in-the-ditch, paper piecing, batting, appliqué, and suggestive sounding words like strip piecing, bargello, and trapunto.

• Your monthly budget has a new category cryptically called *Miscellaneous Needs.*

• Your quilting room *or* studio starts having cupboards and boxes labeled, "Do Not Touch."

• Your *quilter* starts sorting the mail.

• Your *quilter's* computer calendar is password protected.

• A second mortgage suddenly appears on the house without your knowledge as the fabric stash mysterically has increased.

• The new sewing or quilting machine has been given a name.

• She starts talking about her stash like its a member of the family.

   These are just a few of the signs to look for. I am sure there are many others. If it is any consolation when your quilter joins this secret society there are a few things you will never have to worry about. She will be far too busy to be sucked into an Am-Way meeting or run for city council. You on the other hand may have more time alone than before. You may even have enough time to read all of your junk mail.

OH LOOK HONEY! YOUR BIRTHDAY IS ON
THE SAME DAY AS THE QUILTING CONVENTION!
LUCKY YOU!

PARADISE VACATION

everal years ago The Quilter and I found ourselves on our way to Hawaii, without the kids. We had a glorious seven days planned at the extraordinary Grand Wailea Resort on the isle of Maui. Having never been to Maui, we look forward with much anticipation to this time together, we were not disappointed.

The resort and spa were beyond our imagination. A lavish room overlooking the pristine blue waters of the Pacific. Awe inspiring sunsets of brilliant oranges, reds, and yellows. Candle lit dinners, consisting of the freshest catch of day while being bathed by the warmth of a tropical breeze. Early morning runs on the beach and late night moon lit strolls hand in hand. Day trips to various locations; the Hana coast, snorkeling off the Trilogy, and many visits to the numerous art galleries of Lahina.

It was also in this tropical retreat that I promised that I would not allow my work to interrupt our week of paradise, with the exception of a day trip to Oahu for a quick business meeting.

For the most part, I held true to my promise. Unfortunately, I did not make the same request from The Quilter. To her delight, an event occurred on that day trip that would ignite the fire of The Quilter and bring "it"to life. It was just like a sci-fi movie when someone presses the wrong button and releases the mutant creature. Little did I know that The Quilter would soon be awoken, ON OUR VACATION!

On my way to my previously arranged appointment we discussed the various activities for the day which included a trip to the Pearl Harbor Memorial. She would take the tour during my meeting.

After completing the solemn experience of Pearl Harbor she

saw a sign hanging from a light post with an announcement, "Hawaiian Quilt Show next right."

The button had been pushed. The vacation was over. The Quilter surfaced and a right turn ensued.

We returned to Maui that evening with a resolve to create a quilt memorializing the 2,403 Americans killed during the attack on Pearl Harbor. As the evening progressed, I thought I had escaped with only a minor episode of quilter's fever.

How silly of me to think that this would pass that quickly. Planning was in full swing as we boarded our flight back to Maui. The initial quilt design and the fabric needed was scribbled on an Hawaiian Airlines cocktail napkin. The time that would be needed to complete this project was also declared.

The next day I was convinced that the quilting episode had passed. The morning was spent enjoying the ocean. My paradise was still intact and life was very very good.

I'm not sure what happened next. It might have been over-exposure to the sun and sea air because all of a sudden I found that there had been a slight deviation from the planned afternoon activity. Guess where? Correct! The Fabric Warehouse on the Hana Highway in the beautiful island paradise of Maui, Hawaii.

"You know, we can't get Hawaiian fabric on the mainland like we can get here on Maui and it will only take a few minutes."

"Yes dear," was the only feasible response I could come up with at the time, as I stood there in complete disbelief. I could feel it all slipping away...Paradise Lost!

Now, if any of you have ever gone into the fabric or quilt store with your quilter, you know that it is impossible to make a quick in and out stop especially at a store they have never been into. And for heaven sakes at each shop there is always some new project that just has to be purchased. Its not like that there are already 10 plus projects waiting at home.

"But I may never be back here on Maui again, it's not like I can just run on over and pick something up ..."

On this vacation some 5,000 miles away from home in what was once a paradise retreat, I found myself mindlessly wandering through bolts of the most brilliant Hawaiian fabric prints in the world. I am not sure how many bolts of fabric I carried to the cutting table that day, but my arms ached. Is there such thing as Fabric Elbow or Bolt Back?

A thought. Maybe there is a way to claim some medical condition from my doctor so that I can not enter a quilt or fabric store again.

After lugging many bolts of fabric to the cutting table, in my supportive- I'll be glad to help – I hope I can get out of here soon attitude, a question pierced me through the heart from the cutting-table employee (she should be described as the *accomplice*). "How many yards?"

What caught me off guard and still does to this day is *The Look* in The Quilter's eye as she ponders that question. You know, *The Look*, along with the inquisitive pursing of the lips. You can actually see her brain working, "I am thinking of a number," is almost audible. Her quilting brain has fully engaged to determine how much of this particular fabric needs to be purchased. I think in many cases *The Look* indicates, "I wonder how much I can get away with." I am also convinced that *The Look* may be an act. There is no calculating at all! They already know what they need. "A yard and a forth, will be fine."

The finality of *The Look* is one of a pleasurable gleam. The triumph of having found the exact piece of quality fabric and purchasing just the right amount is quite a victory, and the last part of *The Look* reflects that. This part of *The Look* is actually more like *The Little Mermaid* who just scored another thing-a-ma-bob to go with her 20 others.

Although this process only takes a very few moments, I was

caught off guard by what happened after a few pieces had been cut. I think it is a very well thought out plan by The Quilter to do just that, catch me off guard.

The Question – *The Question* usually appears right after the first bolt is cut and *The Look* of satisfaction has just started to fade. *The Question* is designed to make you feel like part of the whole process and in some sick way that you were all for it.

The Question starts out something like this, "Honey what do you think, 7/8 of a yard?"

It's a Quilter's trap, don't be fooled. For me this is beyond my realm of thinking. Not to mention that it is a loaded question. Is there a good answer at all?

First, I am not sure I even know what 7/8 of a yard looks like. It's not like I carry around a yard stick and can say, "Oh, yes dear, 34 inches will do nicely." (Although it may not be a bad idea to have at least a measuring tape handy now and again.)

Second, if I ask the obvious question, "What are you using this for?" This opens me up for a continuous dialogue and conversation surrounding the next quilting project. I don't know if I would want to subject myself to that.

The only answer seems to be, "Yes Dear, sounds good to me." Which, if I am not mistaken, is the confirmation, the stamp of approval, that the two hours in the Fabric Warehouse, was indeed a wonderful experience? The product, process and ultimate purchase was memorable and enjoyable. Memorable? Yes. Enjoyable? The jury is still out.

If you have had this experience on vacation you know that it just doesn't end with the final purchase and "Aloha" as you leave the shop. It also now requires you to figure out how you are going to get the spoils home to the studio. Well lucky for us, there is always a Wal-Mart store located somewhere in the general vicinity of anywhere. I have found that an extra large duffle bag, $19.97, purchased at Wal-Mart saves you a lot of extra time in trying to figure out how to get 35 pounds of fabric and projects in your roll-on suitcase along with your clothes. You also end up with a great collection of duffle bags.

The fun didn't stop here on this trip. After returning from this glorious vacation, we gathered as a family around the suitcases and duffle bag. Children just know that a parent will naturally feel guilt for leaving them for over a week and will consequently shower them with gifts.

We began to pull out our collection of trinkets and surprises for each of our children; a book from Hawaii, shells, pictures of the resort, and T-shirts (don't all parents bring home T-shirts). Everyone was happy.

Then the look of horror from the two older boys as their mother, The Quilter gave them some fabric for some new shorts as one of their gifts from Hawaii. This look was price-less and depicts the look of many a quilters' spouse after one trip with them to the fabric store.

As The Quilter unpacked her duffle bag of fabric, I saw a look of complete satisfaction. It was then that I realized that she had not left paradise 5,000 miles away. To her, paradise was right here.

MY WIFE MAKES ALL OF THESE, BUT DINNER
IS USUALLY MADE BY THE COLONEL OR A CLOWN

Moving Out, Moving In, Moving Up

During our career we have found ourselves with opportunities to move to many different regions of the United States, from large metropolises on the West Coast to small towns in the Southeast. Each move has had different challenges and opportunities associated with it. However, wherever we have moved we have always found wonderful friends to associate with along with more quilters than I ever thought existed.

Those of you that have had similar opportunities realize that there always seems to be additional anxiety, frustration, and frazzled nerves when moving. For us it was finding the right location. Can we have the type of home we would like? Can we afford the home we want? Will the kids make new friends easily? Can we sell our existing home? What will the people be like? And can we find a home to accommodate all of the quilting stuff?

I recall one of the homes we found in the Southeast was not exactly what we thought we wanted. However, it was amazing how quickly The Quilter changed our minds when we realized that with a small remodeling project, we could turn the unfinished bonus room over the attached garage into a full blown quilting room.

Working with our builder, we created the almost ideal quilting room (to that point.) Over 200 square feet of quilting mania designed to meet The Quilter's every need! A large walk-in closet with built in shelves was completed specifically to hold all the fabric. A new quilting table was purchased to fit perfectly in the space provided. TV and stereo systems were installed for additional entertainment, especially so our 2-year-old daughter could be by Mom.

Little did I know that this exposure created a *Mini Me* of The Quilter. (That's a story for another day. *Help! I Created a Quilter.*) The sixth generation of quilters had begun and was alive and well at 4 years old. This is when she started hand stitching fabrics together. By age 6 she'd pieced together her first quilt on The Quilter's sewing machine. Why don't I think about these things before hand?

Anyway, the room was The Quilter's paradise, the envy of many other quilters in the area. For a while I was the area quilter's hero. I am sure if I would have suggested a statue be erected in my honor, the area quilter's would have raised the money and had it done. It was bliss.

I realized that the old saying, "When Mama is happy, every one is happy," is very true.

In our case, when The Quilter was happy and fulfilled, our piece of the quilting world was heavenly. Unfortunately, that did not last as long as we had hoped. Like many things in life, things were about to change. (Good thing I didn't push the statue thing.) I know. You are thinking, "Why in the world would you change things when all was going so well?"

Well, I guess I am glutton for punishment.

The call came to move to the corporate office, clear across the county. Once again we began, with anxiety and reluctance, the process of getting the home ready to sell. And once again moving brought on additional anxiety, frustration, and frazzled nerves.

We were, however, getting almost good at the whole procedure by now. We found a new home and went through the process of coordinating another move. We set a date, got emotionally prepared, said good-bye to all of our friends and then got busy.

Moving Out

Packing began as we wrapped up dishes and loaded up boxes with all of our belongings. Clothes were packed away by room and marked for easy recognition. Favorite toys were boxed up with loving care for the long haul across the country. Valuables and all of the fragile items were carefully stored and packed with watchful care.

Then The Quilter took over. The move took on a whole new life when we made our way to the quilting room. It didn't look like there was too much to move when the work commenced but as we progressed it seemed like everything started to multiply. Where did all of this stuff come from? Where had *I* been over the last year?

With direction from The Quilter, fabric was placed into protective plastic totes and then loaded into boxes. Thread of every type and color was placed into cartons and marked accordingly. Projects were labeled and notes were made with care denoting where each project was located and in which box.

Batting was placed (crammed when The Quilter wasn't looking) in shipping boxes. Cutting tables were broken down and machines were placed in their respective protective covers. The sewing tables were dissembled and marked so we could remember how they were to be assembled.

Finally after what seemed like hours (which it was) we completed the task. The quilting room had taken more time to pack than the kitchen! Probably with more care too!! The once well organized quilting room was now completely stuffed with boxes.

Once again I stared in awe. "How could we have this much quilting stuff? We were only here for one year!" I thought.

I was amazed at the movers the next day when they patiently walked up and down the stairs countless times carrying the precious cargo of The Quilter.

Finally one of them asked me, while The Quilter was in another room, "What is all this stuff anyway?"

"Quilting stuff," I responded.

A quizzical look appeared on his face. I could see the questions formulating in his head like, "Aren't quilts supposed to be light and fluffy? What's with all of these heavy boxes?"

"Don't ask," was the only way I could respond with out getting into a long discussion. I could have attempted to justify and explain all of the reasons why this had occurred but there was not enough time and we needed to get the van packed.

The packing and loading was completed after a very long day and we were off to a new adventure.

Moving In

Helpful hint: We have found through our multiple moves and experience, that the more detail you put into the packing process, the easier the move-in goes.

For whatever reason moving into a new neighborhood and home has a lot more excitement associated with it than moving out. As the moving van pulls to a stop there is an almost audible relief that your possessions have made it. You are whole again. This was even more apparent for The Quilter when the first box marked *quilting room* came off the truck.

There was a challenge with this new home that had been discussed prior to the moving van arriving. We had four bedrooms and an office to put three children, us (the parents), an office, and a quilting room into. Five rooms, six rooms needed. On this occasion the quilting room became the compromise. Which is to say that the quilting room did not get the largest space.

Our boys shared one bedroom which later became known in our family as the "dump".

The down-sized quilting room was laid out with care so that every inch of this small room would be utilized by The Quilter. The boxes slowly began to make their way into the empty house. Directions were given at the front door as items and boxes were moved from the van into the various rooms.

"Kitchen, upstairs bathroom, quilt room, master bedroom, garage, quilt room . . ." The van began to empty and our house was becoming a home, one box at a time.

Half-way through the day, one of the movers approached my wife with a perplexed looked on his face and said, "Ma'am, ah, the room for your quilting stuff, is completely full. Where would you like us to put the rest?"

Her face filled with fear at the thought as we raced up the stairs. A quick look at the room revealed that literally another box would create an avalanche of quilting stuff and the machines and tables were not off the truck yet. The only tragedy of the move so far!

You may ask how I got through this. Well, the conversation went something like this, as we stood in front of that stuffed room while the workers began to stack the boxes in other locations.

"You know this isn't going to work," The Quilter said.

"Yes Dear," was my feeble reply.

"We are going to have to finish the basement!" She stated triumphantly. Translation: *I need to have a larger area.* You notice it is no longer a room, it has become an *AREA*.

My only available response, "Yes Dear."

An area is not easily defined. It could mean something as large as the *area* north of San Francisco. Or it could be as small as the *area* in my head that was now throbbing.

A finished basement would be nice. A reasonable *area* for The Quilter and a nice sized recreation room for the family. Maybe a bedroom or two. Everybody wins. Right?

"So...how much of the basement would you like?"
I cringed and waited for the inevitable pronouncement, "*All of it!*"
She didn't say it, though. She is much smarter than that.
There was to be a long negotiation process involving some
twisted quilting logic that I am sure they teach to quilters
who belong to the *Secret Society of Quilters*.
We discussed what we should do with our unfinished space
and made plans for the construction to begin in the Spring.
A compromise had been tentatively reached. Soon the quilter
would have a new *area* all to herself. The Quilter looked at all
of the newly proposed space, however, and then slowly and
surely she drew her plans against me.
I must have been caught in a weak moment one evening
several weeks later as The Quilter and I discussed purchasing a
new machine for her new area. The last time this had happened
it was several thousand dollars for a Pfaff sewing machine. I
knew that some of the newer more sophisticated machines were
not cheap but would provide The Quilter additional abilities to
enhance her talents. Plans were laid, a savings plan was initi-
ated, and pennies were pinched over the next several months.
(I know, I know, I'm whipped.) I didn't even know what kind of
machine we were saving for yet.
The conversation continued one evening, "You know with the
extra room we will have, we should look at getting a long-arm
quilting machine."
Now I should have clued in on this, but I didn't. I had no
idea what a long-arm quilting machine was. Our ever-evolving
remodeling plan was now to move the boys to their own rooms
in the basement. Also, as a further compromise, the large
dumping room that the boys occupied was to become *additional*
space for The Quilter. A new machine seemed OK so that The
Quilter could have a machine in each room without having to
move them back and forth.

After agreeing, (Never just agree! That was my first fatal flaw,) we further discussed the layout and conversion from the "dump" to the expanded quilting room.

While looking at the layout, The Quilter said, "You know, a long-arm machine will not fit in here."

I am thinking, "What? Are your crazy? This room is three times larger than what you have now."

I didn't say anything, however, as I had this terrible feeling rising from my stomach. I knew that I had gotten into something that I had no idea about.

It must have been the look of bewilderment on my face because The Quilter quickly said, "I need a space 18 feet long and 7 feet wide to operate a long arm machine."

"What?" Blurted from my mouth before I could control what I was saying.

I soon found myself on the internet looking at a behemoth of a machine. This thing was a monster, not to mention that I really hadn't planned on spending the equivalent of the national budget of a small country on a long-arm quilting machine. I had no idea that a long-arm machine was an industrial-size full-blown quilting machine. My home would truly become a light manufacturing facility. Would we have to get special zoning to have such a machine?

I am sure that you have figured out by now that the basement was quickly redesigned to include a quilting studio. The plans of The Quilter had come to fruition. Four hundred feet of quilting bliss was laid out and built to accommodate Big Bertha, the Long-Arm Quilting Machine.

We had moved out, moved in, and The Quilter had *moved up*. Once again peace and bliss entered into our home. The Quilter was happy.

I GUESS HIS WIFE'S QUILTING HOBBY GOT OUT OF HAND

An Awakening

Have you ever been awakened from a deep sleep, not sure where you really are? There's a fog blanketing your mind that does not allow you to process normally, creating a brief moment of panic. This has happened to me on a few occasions when I have had a heavy travel schedule and have been in different time zones and multiple cities within a few days. The worst feeling is when you are suddenly awakened by a terrible dream. You know the kind. You believe that it was only a dream but it's just real enough that you are not quite sure. Reality mixed with some sort of weird fantasy.

Several months ago this exact experience happened to me while I was at home. I was so far removed in a deep sleep I was not sure what I was experiencing. I thought I had heard the alarm ringing. My eyes slowly flickered open, but only for a brief moment. All seemed in order. I knew it was early as is was still dark outside. The home was quiet as it should be at that time of morning and I could hear The Quilter's steady rhythmic breathing next to me. The anxiety flash passed as quickly as it had surfaced and I was soon comfortably slumbering.

I am not sure what awoke me again that morning. But the suddenness threw me off. There was an unnatural light in my bedroom along with what seemed to me a muffled, muted conversation.

I wondered, as I attempted to shake the fog from my mind, "Did one of the children get up and I not hear them. Had a phone call come in that I hadn't heard? What could it be?"

Slowly my mind began to focus. As I turned in bed, I noticed that The Quilter was no longer prone in slumber but sitting upright in bed.

"What could be wrong?" My mind suggested. "Was she sick?

Was someone else sick? Couldn't she sleep? The second thing I focused on was the eerie unnatural light coming from the general direction of the television. I knew that I was sleepy, but I could not figure out what was going on. I glanced at the clock on the night stand. It read 5 a.m.! By now, only having woke up 30 seconds ago, I was beyond confused.

Then I heard the comforting whisper of The Quilter, "Go back to sleep. It's early."

She must of have seen the exasperated look on my face, because again she soothed, "Everything is fine. . . Go back to sleep." Which I promptly and obediently did.

What seemed to be a only few minutes later, my alarm awoke me as light poured into our room. It was time to get ready for work. As I showered that morning, I vividly remember thinking, "What a strange dream."

Dismissing it as such, I kissed The Quilter goodbye as she lay dozing and said, "You ok?"

The muffled, "Yeah. Why'd you ask?" came from under the covers.

"Oh nothing," I whispered. "Just a strange dream."

Nothing was ever mentioned of the incident until the next week when the same thing happened *again.* It happened almost exactly has it had happened the previous week.

This time the fog was not as thick as when The Quilter affectionately said, "Go back to sleep. It's early." I knew it wasn't a strange dream. It was worse. The Quilter was sitting up in bed watching something on T.V. My only confusion was that The Quilter seldom watched television. You know, with all of the projects taking priority.

On this morning, however, she was definitely watching something on the television and very intently may I add. I decided that I needed to see what was so important at 5:07 a.m. that The Quilter didn't even hear me stirring. Reaching for my glasses on the night stand, I sat up.

The Quilter, gave me a slight sheepish smile, which appeared to say, "Sorry I woke you."

I smiled back out of habit. My smile soon diminished when I glanced toward the television. There in front of my sleep filled eyes at 5:08 in the morning was some overly cheerful women holding brightly colored fabric... QUILTS!!

Looking back at my wife in complete disbelief and rubbing the sleep from my eyes, I was attempting to come up with the proper thing to say, when The Quilter spoke first.

"Look it's Nancy, on a quilting show on HGTV!"

I am thinking really hard by now, "Nancy?. . . Nancy? . . . Nancy who? I don't know a Nancy."

As the quilter began to turn up the volume, this person The Quilter is calling Nancy is being interviewed by another cheerful lady discussing something in Quilter's Tongue while holding a brightly colored quilted piece of fabric. I know by now that I must be a having a nightmare.

There is no way that I could actually be sitting in my bed at 5 a.m. with some quilting show blaring at me. Tell me that it isn't possible that two chipper women that I don't even know chatting about fabric and quilting have invaded my sleep. I am sure that I will wake up at any moment and realize this was a bad dream. Unfortunately, this bad dream was reality.

In my bewildered state of being, The Quilter turned to me as a commercial was discussing some new gadget, "I heard about this show from someone at the last guild meeting."

Now in my current state of being, all I could think was, "What have I done to deserve this torture?"

It's bad enough that quilting fills my waking hours, but now it is invading my dreams! What kind of lunatic would put a quilting show on at 5:00 a.m.???

By now I am really concerned for the mental health of my

wife. I am starting to think that this quilting thing is more like a cult. After all, isn't sleep deprivation a key tool cults use to wear you down? And the constant indoctrination! Every time I turn around there is something else happening that is tied into quilts, quilting, quilt guilds, quilt meetings, and quilting bees. Now they are spreading their gospel of colored fabric and thread on TV. Is nothing sacred?

I now know that my attitude must have been affected by the hour of the morning. Quilters are not a cult. They are worse. They are fanatics. They are worse than college football tailgaters in the SEC. Why, you ask? Well, for one thing they aren't cooking up bratwurst and chili. No! They are making beautiful blankets that you are supposed to SLEEP UNDER at 5:00 a.m.! But they can't just *do that* and let it be. They have to wake up at this unearthly hour and see how it is done.

How many individuals do you know, that after watching some new technique discussed, at oh...dark-thirty, on some TV show can't wait to try what they just learned? That's right, after viewing this program, The Quilter quickly arose, turned on the lights, blinding me for a moment, threw on her robe and headed for the bedroom door.

She stopped for a moment and looked at me. I didn't need to say anything. I had the "you've got to be kidding" look going strong.

"What?" The Quilter shot back. With a hand on her hip, she responded, "Didn't you see?"

I knew much better than to answer this question with the obvious, "See what?"

I just let it go, knowing I was going to get the correct answer whether I wanted it or not.

By now The Quilter was speaking just as *chipperly* as Nancy, "I've got to try what they were talking about. I have never seen appliqué done so easily!"

Looking around in utter confusion, I wanted to say, "It is still dark outside... You are whacked!"

But being the supportive husband, I said nothing but, "Please turn out the light and turn off the TV."

I pulled my warm, fluffy, and inviting quilt over my head and slowly faded back to sleep.

GUESS WHAT HONEY! THEY NAMED THE NEW WING
OF THE QUILT STORE AFTER ME!

THE STASH

Recently I told a college of mine that I was working on a book entitled *"Help! I Married a Quilter."* He just laughed and gave me a look that told me, "I am *also* married to a quilter and the title of your book is all I need to hear."

He knew me well enough to know that I would be leaving no stone unturned in my little treatise on the joys of being married to a quilter. "So how big is your wife's stash?" he finally ventured.

"Oh, I don't know," I said. "I think I would have rather had that new 3 Series BMW than a room full of fabric."

"Only a 3 Series? he mocked. "You're lucky. I could have had an S Series Mercedes."

We may have been exaggerating, but I am not entirely certain. I have feared taking an actual inventory of my wife's fabric stash. It is, after all, one of her most prized possessions. It is also one the most bizarre of all quilting traits that us *Goners* see in our quilters.

The *"Stash"* as it is called by most quilters is a collection of fabric which may or *may not* be used someday in the construction of a future quilt project. The stash is added to on a regular basis and its size and variety is used as a status symbol among quilters.

The Quilter told me about a woman she knows who has a very large room dedicated to her stash. Its called *The Tub Room* because all of her fabric is sorted by color and style and stored in large plastic tubs that are stacked from floor to ceiling against each wall and in several rows in the middle of the room.

Once or twice a year her daughters will come over for a week or two and make as many quilts as possible from her stash for charity. Each time they come back, however, the stash is bigger! I am sure that each daughter is hoping to add mom's stash to their own someday.

Every self-respecting quilter has a very detailed system to the stash. It is always stored in a orderly fashion that only The Quilter understands. Sorting by color is only the start.

I am told that a reasonable stash must have every shade of white for a start. Then each color must be laid out in an infinite variety of shades and patterns. Beyond color separation is type of fabric. There are the Batik fabrics which are very popular. Then there are the period reproduction fabrics. Civil War reproductions are very sought after and must have their own section. Then there are the ethnic and cultural prints. These are fabrics from specific countries or areas of the world that have their own unique patterns and colors. This is why traveling with a quilter is guaranteed to result in several new fabrics for the stash.

The best stashes have fabric from all over the world and from multiple sources. You can't replace a stash by going to the nearest fabric store. This is why a stash starts to have a life of its own. The stash becomes an extension of The Quilter!

I am trying to think of what I have that is the equivalent to a stash but I can't think of anything. I don't overstock things that exceed what I can use in three to four lifetimes. I guess that the only thing that would compare might be someone who buys an entire library of books that they never intend to read. My wife will insist, however, that every piece in her stash is important.

My wife relates the story of Eunice, an octogenarian in her quilt guild who is attempting to deplete her stash before she dies. She pieces together quilt after quilt and then lets the guild finish them. They are auctioned for charity and are gifted to the deserving in the community. No one really believes that she will finish off her stash but they all admire her for trying.

No one understands the importance of the stash to a quilter like quilting fabric stores. Oh, they are conniving and vicious. They prey on quilters like fast-food stands feed on the hungry. They know that quilters are helpless to resist their wares. They create the most novel excuses to bring quilters to their stores. But when has a quilter really needed an excuse?

There's the block of the month club, quilting classes, guild meetings, and even state-wide quilt shop hops. They know that if a quilter walks through the door, yards of fabric and the newest gadget will be walking out the door minutes later. After all who walks into McDonalds and says, "No thanks. I'm just looking."

Nothing signals the need to add to the stash than when you have made a withdrawal. It is at that point that you must replenish the stash equal to the amount that was removed and then add to it some more. A good stash never stays the same size or gets smaller. It must continue to multiply.

Sometimes quilters think that their addiction can be appeased by opening their own quilt shop. That doesn't ever work because their personal stash just grows bigger *faster*. The store isn't their stash. A stash is definitely NOT for sale. A quilt store owner, unless completely controlled by an in house accountant who is not a quilter, will just spend all of the profits on their own supplies. I can just hear the conversation now, "But honey, since I own my own store I can buy everything at wholesale!"

The only time quilters are generous with their stash is during times of crisis. When the call goes out that Timbucthree just had an earthquake and needs 10,000 quilts, quilters will dive into their stash and knock out a dozen quilts each in as many days without having to waste one minute at a quilt store. After all, when the crisis is over, half the fun is building the stash back up, and up some more.

Unfortunately building the stash often leads to the purchase of new machines and gadgets. Quilt and fabric stores often put their hardware right up front so that you have to walk past them before getting to the fabric.

A quilter can walk by that new computerized sewing machine or quilting machine only so many times before curiosity sets in. She will eventually look. Then she will receive a demonstration. It will then become a definite want, something that would be very convenient to have. It starts gnawing on her. Every time she goes to the quilt shop to add to the stash the machine starts to call her... by name. A bond is formed. She must have this machine. It is now a need. You must now make all necessary financial arrangements.

A quilter's stash will always outlive her and every quilter will make arrangements for who will take care of her stash. It will be in the will or be made part of a living trust. Will the stash stay in one piece? Or will she divide it among children and fellow quilters to become a part of their individual stashes. These are very important questions that need to be answered. You should consult your legal advisor on the matter sooner rather than later.

My colleage from the beginning of this chapter shared a few stories with me about his quilter's stash and we had a pretty good laugh. He then suggested we might get together for dinner with our wives. I gave him a look that suggested he must have lost his mind for suggesting we introduce our quilters over dinner.

He thought about it for a moment and said, "You're right. Bad idea. Good luck with your book."

THE TRIALS OF A TRAVELER

I travel quite a bit for business and as many travelers do, I have often find myself at many airports awaiting flights. I have been delayed too many times to keep track of, and I have been stuck in my share of security lines "patiently" waiting and hoping that I will make my flight.

On one of these occasions I found myself booked on a very early morning flight to Seattle, Washington. I would be working with one of our largest customers on a critical project that would potentially bring millions of dollars of new business to our company. I was still working through several key pieces of information in my mind when I found myself in an incredibly long security line at 6:00 a.m. at Denver International.

As I wound my way through the endless switchbacks, it began to feel like I was waiting in a line at *Disney World*. Using this useless time, I went through the various questions, concerns, and suggestions in my mind as I rehearsed solutions for our customer over and over. As I neared the front of the security line my focus was lost for a moment as a small ruckus erupted from the far side of security. I noticed a lady with a very brightly colored tote bag draped over her arm being stopped by security, indicating a secondary screening was necessary.

Now you may not think that this scene would be out of the ordinary and you are probably right. But then my life isn't ordinary. Despite the fact that I had just lost all of my concentration, I began to smile as I came close enough to hear what was going on. This poor woman with her patchwork quilted tote bag was also lugging another innocuous over-sized bag. To the experienced eye, however, this was definitely not just a bag, it was her sewing machine!

My smile widened and I chuckled as the quilter was being detained by security and was being forced to unpack her sewing machine and her entire tote bag. For once, it wasn't me with my quilter! Grabbing my bag off the security belt I could hear the quilter excitedly pulling from her bag various projects and explaining to the very patient security officer about each one in detail.

She hadn't even unpacked her sewing machine and all the gadgets she probably had lugged along as I hustled off to make my flight. Inwardly, I hoped that she didn't have a tight schedule. With a sigh of relief that it wasn't me packing the sewing machine along this time, I boarded the tram to head for my concourse. I quickly forgot the incident and focused back on the important events of the day ahead.

Making the flight wasn't as challenging as I thought. We had a bit of a delay. Imagine that! Being hustled aboard and seated toward the back of the plane, I found to my joy that I was the only one on my row. It's a traveler's dream next to being asked to give up your seat for a first class seat up front.

I grabbed my presentation and began intently going through each page methodically, thinking of various questions or objections and how I could handle each. Completely lost in this thought process I was unaware that our plane had not moved from the gate. Time passed; for once my mind was too engaged in thought to worry about the time. However, the restlessness around me soon brought me back to the here and now. I found that it had been 20 minutes since the last person boarded. Without too much worry, I got back to more important things.

The delay was giving me some extra preparation time. As time passed, I thought I recognized through the background noise a familiar sound. Not wanting to look away from my important document I pushed the noise out of my mind. But the noise became louder to the point that ignoring it was not possible. Slowly I raised my head and gazed over the empty seat in front of me. I rubbed my eyes. My mouth gaped open in disbelief. Coming down the isle was, you guessed it, the quilter.

She was still dragging her precious goods.

"Unbelievable," I thought.

The quilter had not stopped to look for any over-head space as she shimmied down the isle. She had her machine in tow and was knocking into other passengers with her struggles to keep her balance. She was busily speaking and greeting anyone that looked her way or apologizing for holding up the plane as she looked for her seat. She continued in my direction moving closer and closer to the back of the plane. The voice in my head was like those slow motion scenes in the movies, "Nooooooooooooooo."

I put my head down to avoid being seen and shook my head in disbelief. My perfect flight was coming undone. Frantically, as if my life depended on it, I searched for any open seat away from the quilter. Even a middle seat would be better than the torture of two plus hours discussing the quilter's projects whether finished or not yet started.

As she moved closer, my mind switched to full defense mode. I began thinking of various excuses that could allow me to finish preparing my presentation. I could fake hearing loss, pretend I didn't know English, or just ignore her rudely. With my luck I would probably find that she knew My Quilter. They were probably in the same quilt guild.

Luckily she stopped one row short and took the open seat in front of me. Standing, I quickly and quietly assisted the quilter in stowing her precious cargo in the overhead bins as the plane gently rocked backward and pulled away from the gate. Salvation! The quilter was safely stowed and seated. I breathed a sigh of relief as the loud speaker crackled to life.

"This is your capt'in speaking. If we can get everyone quickly in their seat we will try to make up our lost time this morning."

Taxing quickly down the runway, I was once again engrossed in my work. We climbed with little incident through 10,000 feet as muffed sounds began chatting around me. Tuning out these sounds, like any flight, was easy until I heard a sound I could not tune out. My ear caught the sound of Quilter's Tongue, the distinct language spoken between two quilters sharing their projects and stories.

My first thought was that this poor woman had started talking to herself. Then the blood drained from my face as I realized there were two distinct voices. That meant that there was another quilter on the plane! Sure enough across the isle was the perfect portrait of an elderly grandmother, a Norman Rockwell image to be sure, talking up a raging storm with the quilter in front of me. This was not the kind of turbulence I expected at 37,000 feet. I got the luck of the draw this trip. Not one quilter but two. My concentration was completely gone as I rolled my eyes in disbelief. What a great story The Quilter would hear tonight.

Their conversation cut through the drone of the plane like a brand new pair of Gingher Scissors through an old cotton sheet. I soon found out that the reason for our delay was that the security officer was a quilter and was more than eager to see all the quilter's projects. The gate agent was also a quilter and had held the plane when she heard from the security officer who just happened to be in her guild. I would not have been surprised if I found out that the pilot was married to a quilter, and also in their guild. There was absolutely NO escape for me. I gave up. I got comfortable. I closed my eyes and drifted off to sleep as an excited discussion began about trapunto. I thought trapunto was an Italian dish. Wrong again, even at 37,000 feet.

MY HOME OWNERS INSURANCE JUST DOUBLED. THEY FOUND
OUT THAT MY WIFE'S FABRIC STASH WAS WORTH MORE THAN THE HOUSE

HELP! I MARRIED A QUILTER...
AND THEN...

I have spent my entire married life surrounded by and inundated with quilters and quilting stuff. I have wondered why I have been able to hold my own...well at least until now. Before you jump to conclusions and think that I have gone completely off the deep end by starting my own stash and buying my own machine just to get even with The Quilter, let me assure you that I have not. In fact, I have yet to use a sewing machine, serger, or long-arm quilting machine. I can't recall even threading a needle recently. I have, however, carried many quilting and sewing machines of all sorts, shapes and sizes. But I have not used one to stitch, bind, or create any part or portion of a quilt.

Despite all of the above efforts, I have nonetheless, tragically become personally infected with the quilting virus. Here is my unbelievable but true story.

I have spent my entire professional career working with companies and brands to enhance their market position and increase their sales. I have worked with companies large and small, from the intimate Mom and Pop operations to the most aggressive retailers in the world. I have thrived on the competition and the challenges of the market place, finding new and innovative ideas and products to produce and sell.

Each opportunity presented different challenges to overcome. Each time I entered a new job, I was presented with new possibilities that were just waiting to be explored. Each opportunity came with a wide variety of expectations and commitments. This was my world away from The Quilter and in this world I felt comfortable and in charge.

From 2000–2004, I was part of the management team of a large company in Denver, Colorado. Due to the great success of our team, the company was soon ripe for sale. A larger company eventually made an offer, the sale was made, and everybody was happy. The Quilter and I, however, found ourselves looking for a new adventure.

We were anxious to get started so we began to explore the many new options that began to surface. Although none of them were the perfect fit, each was carefully evaluated. I was willing to be at home and watch The Quilter at work for only a very brief time before I started getting stir-crazy or should I say stitch-crazy. Feeling the need to keep myself busy, I found myself commuting to Salt Lake City, Utah, helping to run a small manufacturing group.

Then it happened! Without warning, the call came. The conversation went something like this.

"Hello?"

A calm, mellow voice answered confidently and said, "Hello. We understand that you have some very unique talents and abilities and we would like to discuss them with you at your earliest convenience."

I was a bit caught off guard as I stumbled and stammered with my response, "Um, sure, ah, I am not sure I caught your name."

An intentional pause occurred. I could almost hear a smile spread across his face, knowing that he had me off my guard.

The voice, polite but firm responded, "I don't believe I gave you my name, but a mutual acquaintance, *Laurel*, gave us your name and contact information."

I had learned in that quick exchange that there was more than one person behind this phone call. Now what? My mind began to race frantically through all my professional contacts; companies I had worked for, individuals I had met, retailers we sold to, and even the people I had fired. But no *Laurel* registered. Nothing, zip, zilch, zero.

Trying to play it cool and knowing that the next move was mine, I somewhat less confidently than before said, "That's great. What can I help you with?"

"Can you come and visit with us tomorrow afternoon about an opportunity we think that might just fit you perfectly?" came the direction.

I was still a bit perplexed but my interest was peaked, I must admit. I quickly glanced through my calendar. I could see clearly that I was available.

Not willing to submit to this meeting without some more information or clear direction and thinking that I would catch *them* off guard, I quickly asked, "It appears that I can move some things around to accommodate you. May I request *what* you would like me to be prepared with?"

Without the slightest pause, the response was fired back, "No need. We already have what we need and we would just like to get to know you better."

I was stunned to silence when I heard that they had what *they* needed. What about what *I* need? I was given an address and time to meet as my mind raced ahead trying to figure out who *Laurel* was.

What I had done or not done to deserve this call and what was the *opportunity*? I came to my senses long enough to write down the information I was given.

"Oh," the voice added with finality. "Remember to ask for Jason."

As pleasantries and salutations were exchanged but not registering in my racing mind, I thought forward to the following day. I was not comfortable going into any meeting with so little information. Attempting to put the call behind me I was quickly brought back to reality when a problem that needed solving needed some attention.

Later that night I reflected again and again on the conversation earlier in the day. "What could this opportunity be? How did they really get my contact information? Who was this Laurel that they referred to and how come I could not place her?"

Mulling these and other thoughts over and over in my mind I drifted off to a restless sleep.

The appointed time ominously approached as I drove to a nearby office complex. I noted that the address was correct and checked in with the office security. I made my way down the hall quickly and stopped by the office register on the wall. I scanned the names of the companies located in the building. Nothing there registered, nor could I associate any of the companies to a *Laurel*.

The only names that appeared on the register were law firms, financial groups, and equity firms; names like *Smith, Johnson, Jones & Partners, Smith & Barney, and Ethan & Company.* The *"us"*, I was suppose to meet with was also there, fourth floor corner office.

The appointed time had arrived. Quickly moving into the elevator I hit #4 and headed to that floor. I think my stomach stayed on the first floor. I exited the elevator and headed to the corner office to seek out the mystical opportunity that had been mentioned less than 24 hours earlier.

I walked into the foyer of the modestly decorated office. I was greeted by the friendly but not recognizable face of the receptionist.

"Mr. Hyland."

This was a statement not a question.

"Jason is waiting for you in the conference room. Please follow me."

Without hesitation I followed the receptionist down the corridor to the large conference room. There I finally met the voice on the phone. Jason.

We exchanged pleasantries as others gathered. Yes others.

The *us* turned into several people. Not only was I in the dark, I was seriously outnumbered.

Each individual introduced themselves as they entered the room, greeting me with a warm, firm handshake. No one was introduced as *Laurel* though. Hmmm...The conversation settled down as they began to ask several casual questions concerning my background and experience. This was just for reference of course.

I tried to answer each question clearly. I was still in the dark but I could see we were coming to the real point of our conversation. They were getting ready to reveal the *"opportunity."*

"We understand that your wife is a quilter," Jason stated matter-of-factly.

I was caught completely off guard.

"Yes," I stammered, wondering what in the world kind of question was this was. Had they looked into The Quilter's background too?

The next phrase stole my breath away as I felt the walls closing in, frantically looking for a quick escape route if this conversation turned ugly.

"We hear that you understand the quilting world and how the quilter's mind works, seeing that you are married to a quilter and having been associated with many quilters throughout your life. Is that correct?"

"What are they asking?" Is this some kind of undercover quilter's sting? Could I be on *Candid Camera*?" I quickly looked around the room to see if this really was a joke.

I am sure they saw in a split second the terror in my eyes. Even though I was attempting to hold my professional composure, my brain was screaming almost audibly:

"Quilting, you have got to be kidding! I live with a quilter but I AM NOT A QUILTER by any stretch of the imagination. How dare you!"

Gathering my wits about me and calming my very troubled mind, I began to formulate my witty response. All of those years of training from The Quilter took complete control as I uttered, *"Yes, De* .. um, . . Yes. I'm married to a quilter."

I was in shock. What had happened to my witty response? Ouch!

"This was not good," I thought.

I smiled as if nothing out of the ordinary had occurred. Quilting questions are always answered by "Yes Dear." My stomach, in the meantime, was kicking up a mighty fine brew of acid reflux.

Could this really be happening? Our conversation continued as I thought, "I am in a board room with some high profile business types discussing *quilting?*" This has to be a dream. I know! I haven't awoken from last night restless sleep yet. I am sure the alarm will be ringing any moment. And there it was, as if right on cue, An ALARM, but not the one I awake to each morning and definitely not the one I would have anticipated.

"We are looking for a new CEO to work with a company we have acquired," Jason said.

"Finally!" I thought. "We're back on track."

I quickly settled in to hear what these professionals had in mind, even though deep down warning alarms were still sounding.

"The opportunity that we would like to further discuss with you is the potential to become the Chief Executive Officer of *Handi Quilter®,* a leading quilting machine company. *Laurel,* the founder of *Handi Quilter®,* recommended you."

Shocked, would be an understatement as I slowly closed my gaping mouth and attempted to keep my composure. My mind raced. With all the things I had done in my professional career, my primary reference at this meeting was from a *QUILTER!* Who would have thought quilting would have brought me to this? Of all the things . . . a quilting company? I could only imagine what my friends and family would say if I were to even *consider* this job!

As you can guess, I soon found myself fully immersed in the quilting industry as the CEO of *Handi Quilter®*. Work is no longer an escape from quilting. It *is* quilting, quilting shows, new products, quilting retreats, and yes quilts, quilts and more quilts. Quilts are my life now, 24 hours a day.

Yes, my family has had their share of fun and my friends refer to me as Mr. Quilter.

My kids just smile that sarcastic smile that seems to say, "The Quilter got you Dad. She got you good."

I have often wondered, "Was this part of The Quilter's grand plan? Have I been a pawn in her scheme all of this time?"

If so, then I believe that I am married to the **Greatest Quilter of all time**. Not only is she truly a great quilter, she has arranged everything and everyone around her to be centered around quilting. And maybe that isn't bad. If people looked at their family, their neighborhood, and even the world like a quilter, they would see that you can patch together a lot of different and strange looking fabric to form a warm and inviting work of art.

Several years ago, after uttering "Yes Dear" for the first time, I had no idea that I had just married a quilter. But through the years as I look at what quilting has *really* brought to my life and to my family, I can see that being married to a quilter requires no help at all.

THE READING OF THE QUILTER'S WILL

...AND TO MY DAUGHTER SUSAN, I LEAVE MY PFAFF,
ALL OF MY BATIK FABRIC, AND MY CUTTING TABLE.

GLOSSARY

You would think after living with a quilter for several years that I would know everything there is to know about quilting. Unfortunately I only know enough to get myself into trouble. I have yet to make a stitch into a quilt, even though I have seen it done countless times. I am reasonably observant however, so I have picked up a few terms that I think I understand. I have tried to explain the few terms I know below. I realize that my understanding is from an outsiders point of view so please forgive any inaccuracies.

Appliqué – is a French word that somehow is used in American quilting. It describes a technique where you sew one piece of fabric onto another. Quilters use a lot of terms derived from foreign words that automatically make simple things more expensive. Hence you put *appliqué* on *fabriqué*.

Backing – is the fabric used for the bottom layer or backside of a quilt. It also refers to the financial BACKING given to a quilter by her spouse in terms of dollars and long-term credit.

Bargello – is the name of a quilt design which is formed by staggering colors up and down within vertical rows, often forming a design which resembles flames. It is also the design on your dinner after it was left in the oven too long when your quilter was engrossed in her latest project.

Batik – is a method in which fabric is treated with some waxy stuff in random places on the cloth and then dyed to create interesting patterns. It is a lot like a tie-died cloth but 10 times more expensive.

Batting – is a layer of fluffy stuff between a top layer of patch-work and a layer of backing material which provides puffiness and warmth. Think of a Pop Tart. You have a crust on top and crust on the bottom and strawberry "batting" in the middle. It is also called a sandwich. (I am not making this up.)

Bearding – is the process in which the batting fibers of a quilt poke through the top, or bottom, of the quilt via the needle holes. Again think strawberry filling seeping up through the holes on your Pop Tart.

Betweens – refers to small, thin needles, with small eyes, used in hand quilting. It also refers to time spent quilting as in "I always find time to quilt betweens housework".

Bias – is the diagonal of a piece of fabric. A true bias is at a 45 degree angle. It also refers to strong quilting preferences as in "I have a strong bias towards hand quilting over machine quilt-ing". (Or vice-versa.)

Bleeding – refers to what happens when there is too much dye in a fabric so when you wash it the color bleeds onto the other fabric in the quilt. Bleeding is also what happens to your check-ing account when your quilter goes to the quilt store.

A Border – is strips of fabric forming a frame around the quilt top. When asked to help pick out a border color it is smart to pick the ugliest color possible to avoid being asked to help again. If a quilter finds out that you have any color sense at all you will never have peace.

Calico – is a 100% cotton fabric with any small repeated pattern printed on it. Calico is a traditional fabric for old-fashioned quilts. Quilters must have at least a 25 year supply of Calico in their stash at all times.

Cheater's cloth – is a pre-printed fabric with a quilt design printed on the fabric, thus eliminating the tedious task of hand-piecing the quilt. Cheater's cloth was probably invented by a man because he thought (stupidly) that when quilters saw how easy it was then nobody would hand-piece ever again.

Cross hatching – is a grid-like quilting pattern designed to fill in a big space of plain fabric. It is really just a criss-cross pattern that looks a lot like the design on a perfectly grilled steak.

A Cutting mat – is a thick, durable mat which is used with a rotary cutter. It is particularly used to cut multiple layers of fabric in strips and squares. It has lines on it to make measuring easier as well. It was invented after quilters kept destroying every table top in the house.

Directional print – is a piece of fabric that has an obvious directional print. Remember vertical is up and down and horizontal is left and right and one of those directions will make you look taller.

Fat quarter – is a half-yard of fabric, cut down the middle to measure 18" x 22". It is the equivalent of a quarter-yard of fabric but fatter.

Feed dogs – refers to the mechanical teeth under the presser foot area of a sewing machine which move to pull the fabric through the machine. It is also the more personal part of the message on the fridge *"Gone quilting. Feed dogs"*.

Foundation piecing – refers to a method of assembling a quilt block by sewing pieces to a muslin/fabric foundation. This method adds stability to delicate fabrics as well as stabilizing bias and may be called "Crazy Quilting." Actually all quilting can be called "Crazy Quilting."

Foundation paper piecing – is a method of using a paper pattern as a guide for constructing a quilt block. The fabric pieces are sewn right onto the paper using the drawn lines as a guide. It is a lot like origami for quilters.

French double fold binding – really is way too complicated to be defined by me in this book.

Freezer paper appliqué – refers to a method of appliqué in which a pattern/piece is drawn onto the dull side of freezer paper, and then ironed onto the wrong side of the fabric. The freezer paper is then removed after the pieces are sewn together, or to its background foundation. The freezer paper is rendered useless after this process. Freezer paper in the shape of a tulip will not work well for freezing meat.

Griege goods – is fabric straight from the factory that has not been printed on, dyed or treated. It is pronounced "gray goods." I believe you pay extra to have nothing done to this fabric.

Guild – is an organization of quilters in a community who meet on a regular basis to discuss quilting. Quilt guilds hold official meetings for the "Secret Society of Quilters." A good portion of these meetings are spent on spousal manipulation, creative receipt doctoring, and how to use half your food budget for quilting without your husband noticing.

Hand-dyed – is fabric that has been hand dyed. Duh.

Hanging sleeve – is a tube or sleeve sewn on the back top of the quilt in order to hang the quilt for display. This is applied to all quilts that you will never sleep under.

Homespun – refers to fabric that is either hand woven, or made to appear as hand woven, with larger, thicker diameter threads used. The weave tends to be looser. And remember the rule, the older it looks, the more it costs.

Invisible stitch – is a stitch that is created when there is no thread in your needle.

Lap quilting – I know what you're thinking! But lap quilting actually refers to a method of quilting using hoops to complete small portions of the quilt at a time. When a quilter gets hooked on lap quilting they can literally be quilting 90% of the time. They are able to take the quilt anywhere they go. Even a trip to the DMV can be a relaxing experience for a lap quilter.

Loft – refers to the fluffiness of the quilt. If it has high loft it is probably very comfortable to sleep under. If it has low loft it shows off the stitches better. If you are married to serious quilter you will have few fluffy quilts in your house.

Long-arm quilting – refers to a type of machine quilting. A long-arm quilting machine looks a lot like a small John Deer tractor mounted to tracks that move in all directions while it quilts very fast. It gets its name because if you use this machine a lot you will get long arms.

Miniature quilts – refer to very small quilts made of 2"– 3" blocks. They are made by very small quilters.

Muslin – is an un-dyed woven fabric that is often used for quilt backings, background fabric for appliqué, or foundation fabric for crazy quilting. It is available unbleached or bleached. Muslin should not be confused with a dominant Middle-Eastern religion.

Piecing – is the process of stitching together pieces of fabric to create a larger unit. There are multiple techniques for doing this. Piecing together a quilt is step one of the artistic process of making a quilt. The top of the quilt is the canvas and the fabric is the paint.

Sandwich – is a commonly used term and refers to placement of the quilt top, the batting, and the backing together. It is also a common dinner served by a busy quilter.

Stash – is the most used term for a quilter's fabric collection. The size of a quilter's stash is a very important status symbol and is one the quilter's most prized possessions.

Stitch in the Ditch – is a phrase taken from a book by Dr. Suess called, *"The Snitch who Stitched in the Ditch with a Witch,"* but the phrase now means stitching on the seam between two pieces of fabric.

Trapunto – is another foreign word that doesn't mean anything except to quilters. It refers to a dimensional design in a quilt by which closely sewn lines of stitching are stuffed with batting to make them appear 3-dimensional, or raised from the surface and is commonly used in Whole Cloth quilts.

Whole Cloth – refers to a quilt top that is one whole piece of fabric elaborately quilted using various quilting styles, such as trapunto.

Zinger – is a small border added just outside the finished and assembled quilt top and is used to draw attention to the quilt center (add "zing"). A zinger is also a comeback from a quilter to the question, "Are you sure you really need that?"

I am sure that as I hang around The Quilter, and now other quilters through the years, that I will learn several more special words and phrases in Quilter's Tongue. But for now this is all I remember.

Ready Reference

I've tried to explain many quilting terms in the Glossary, however, this quick reference guide is an attempt to clear up any confusion about several commonly misunderstood words in Quilter's Tongue. This guide is especially helpful for non-quilters who may hear this strange language for the first time.

Quilting Term	What It Is...	What It's Not...
Fat Quarter	– a half-yard of fabric, cut down the middle to measure 18" x 22".	– a hamburger combination meal with extra cheese, mayo, and large fries.
Quilting Bee	– a formal gathering of many quilters designed to create a quilt quicker than normal.	– nick name for someone who buzzes around a quilt or fabric shop.
Stitching in the Ditch	– stitching on the seam between two pieces of fabric.	– an off-color joke. Quilters don't tell those kind of jokes!
Batting	– the fluffy material between the quilt top and bottom.	– despite what you think you know, it's not about baseball.

Quilting Term	What It Is	What It's Not
Quilt Block	– pieced material, usually a square.	– a unit of measurement to determine the closeness of a quilt store.
Long Arm Quilting Machine	– industrial quilting machine that stitches specific patterns or allows the quilter to freely create a stitch pattern.	– an inexpensive sewing machine.
Viking	– a quality sewing machine manufacturing company.	– a football team mascot or one bad dude.
Piecing	– sewing a quilt block together.	– eating between meals.
Binding	– stitching the loose edges of the quilt to create a finished edge.	– the act of becoming constipated.
Free Motion	– stitching with a free movement in a nonrepetitive pattern.	– a legal term that proposes an early release from jail.

Quilting Term	What It Is	What It's Not
Bobbin	– a secondary spool of thread in a sewing machine that completes the stitch with the main spool.	– a British Police Officer.
Quick Quilt	– quilt kit that takes less than 6 hours to complete.	– not accurate at all. It is an Oxymoron.
Rotary Cutter	– fabric cutter which allows the quilter to cut fabric by rolling a rotary blade in a straight line.	– a fancy pizza cutter.
Stripping	– sewing fabric together in strips.	– don't even go there.
Basting	– putting large temporary stitches in a quilt to hold it together.	– what Grandma does to the Turkey.
Crazy Quilt	– random pieces of fabric put together from your stash.	– what you want to tell your quilter that her quilt looks like, but don't dare to.
Stack and Whack	– method to create a kaleidoscope type design on a quilt.	– what you do to overgrown shrubs.

Quilting Term	What It Is	What It's Not
Thread Play	– Libby Leahman's method of using specialty threads to create texture in a quilt.	– something the cat does with a ball of yarn.
Thimbleberries	– a popular pattern and fabric design company.	– pie for Thanksgiving.
Log Cabin	– a specific type of quilt block.	– syrup for your waffles.
Sampler	– quilt with all different types of quilt blocks.	– an appetizer assortment.
Scrap Quilt	– quilt made from left over material from one's stash.	– a bunch of rags.